Bruna dos Santos F. de Carvalho

Public civil action and constitutionality control

Bruna dos Santos F. de Carvalho

Public civil action and constitutionality control

From the perspective of the effects of judicial decisions

ScienciaScripts

Imprint
Any brand names and product names mentioned in this book are subject to trademark, brand or patent protection and are trademarks or registered trademarks of their respective holders. The use of brand names, product names, common names, trade names, product descriptions etc. even without a particular marking in this work is in no way to be construed to mean that such names may be regarded as unrestricted in respect of trademark and brand protection legislation and could thus be used by anyone.

Cover image: www.ingimage.com

This book is a translation from the original published under ISBN 978-620-2-03998-7.

Publisher:
Sciencia Scripts
is a trademark of
Dodo Books Indian Ocean Ltd. and OmniScriptum S.R.L publishing group

120 High Road, East Finchley, London, N2 9ED, United Kingdom
Str. Armeneasca 28/1, office 1, Chisinau MD-2012, Republic of Moldova, Europe
Managing Directors: Ieva Konstantinova, Victoria Ursu
info@omniscriptum.com

Printed at: see last page
ISBN: 978-620-8-40688-2

ACKNOWLEDGMENTS

To God for the accomplishment of this work.

To my parents, Euclides and Edilene, for their support.

To my husband, Marco Soares de Carvalho, for his motivation and companionship. To Professor Larissa Clare Pochmann da Silva, for sharing her knowledge in civil procedural law classes, and to all those who trusted my work and contributed in some way to its completion.

"Justice by itself and for itself alone does not exist, it exists only in the form and to the extent that men want it and conceive of it."

Chief Justice of the Supreme CourtJoaquim Barbosa

SUMMARY

This work aims to analyze the subject of Public Civil Action and Constitutionality Control, and consists of finding out whether it is appropriate to use Public Civil Action for Constitutionality Control, with the objective of verifying whether there are possibilities for this institute to take over the exclusive prerogative of the Federal Supreme Court when it comes to assessing the constitutionality of a law or normative act. To this end, in addition to a doctrinal perspective on the institutes of public civil action and constitutionality control, studies were carried out based on doctrinal and jurisprudential research by the Court of Justice of the State of Rio de Janeiro and the Federal Supreme Court. It can be concluded that the Federal Supreme Court has recognized the use of public civil action as a suitable instrument for the incidental control of constitutionality, by diffuse means, of any law or normative act, as long as the constitutional controversy is present in the cause of action and not in the claim, qualifying as a preliminary issue, indispensable to the resolution of the main litigation.

Keywords:

Public Civil Action, Control of Constitutionality, Federal Supreme Court, Usurpation of Jurisdiction.

SUMMARY

1- INTRODUCTION

The Public Civil Action is a topic that has been discussed for some years among jurists, scholars and legal practitioners, in terms of its object, the parties entitled to bring the action and the effect of its sentence, as it brings up new issues, mainly linked to the institutes of active legality and res judicata in the PCA.

Because of the *erga omnes* effects of the judgment in the PCA, some jurists believe that the collective action cannot be used as an instrument of diffuse control of constitutionality, since such effects are proper to the abstract control of constitutionality exercised by the Supreme Court. In this vein, they argue that such effects make the PCA a true substitute for the Direct Action for Unconstitutionality, thus characterizing usurpation of the STF's competence and deviation from the object of the PCA itself.

Based on studies of the case law of the higher courts of the Judiciary, the position is that the use of diffuse control of constitutionality in the PCA is possible as long as the constitutional controversy is in the cause of action and not in the claim itself.

The aim of this work is to analyze whether it is possible to control constitutionality in the Public Civil Action, without usurping the STF's competence with regard to the abstract control of constitutionality. To this end, the method of doctrinal and jurisprudential research will be used, grouping together ideas and concepts that will allow us to reach a general conclusion on the subject.

This monograph is structured in five chapters. In the first two of these, it will deal with the historical question of Public Civil Action and Constitutionality Control, addressing how both institutes arose in the course of legal history.

In the third chapter, we will define the PCA, analyze its purpose and the entities entitled to bring it, as well as the effects of res judicata in the PCA. Furthermore, the analysis will focus on the study of res judicata in collective actions, which is of fundamental importance for clarifying the problem presented here.

The fourth chapter will analyze the system of constitutionality control in Brazil, which, in a peculiar way, provides for both diffuse and concentrated control of constitutionality. The main characteristics of these two types of control will be analyzed, as well as the main ways in which the Supreme Court exercises abstract control of norms in Brazilian law, with emphasis on the different effects of the respective decisions in diffuse and concentrated control.

The fifth chapter, entitled Control of constitutionality in public civil action, discusses the problem that we set out to study here, analyzing doctrinal criticism of the control of constitutionality in the PCA and the understanding of the Superior Federal Court on the matter. More specifically, the question of unconstitutionality as an incidental issue in collective action will also be analyzed, as well as the importance of analyzing the case in order to reach a conclusion on this matter.

2- CONCEPT AND HISTORICAL REFERENCE

2.1 THE FIRST PRECEDENT OF CONSTITUTIONALITY CONTROL

The idea of constitutionality control is linked to the supremacy of the Constitution over the entire legal system and also to constitutional rigidity and the protection of fundamental rights.[1]

Control of constitutionality is therefore a guarantee of the supremacy of the fundamental rights and guarantees laid down in the constitution which, as well as being limits on the power of the state, are also part of the legitimization of the state itself, determining its duties and making the democratic process possible in a state governed by the rule of law.[2]

The first precedent for the control of constitutionality was in 1800 in the case of Marbury v. Madison. When US President John Adams, at the end of his term, passed a law reorganizing the federal judiciary *(the Circuit Court Act),* which created sixteen new federal judgeships. Soon after, in 1801, a new law (*the Organic Act of the District of Columbia)* authorized the President to appoint forty-two justices of the peace, with his Secretary of State, John Marshall, in charge of delivering the investiture acts to the appointees. However, Marshall did not have time to complete the task before the government adjourned, and some of the appointees did not receive them.[3]

The new President, Thomas Jefferson, was sworn in, and his Secretary of State, James Madison, following his lead, refused to hand over the inauguration certificates to those who had not received them. Among the justices of the peace appointed but not sworn in was William Marbury, who filed a *writ of mandamus* in December 1801 to have his right to the office recognized. The request was made

[1] MORAES, Alexandre de. **Constitutional Law.** 21ªEd. Sao Paulo: Atlas, 2007. p. 674.
[2] KELSEN, Hans. **Pure theory of law.** Sao Paulo: Martins Fontes, 1985. p. 288-290.
[3] BARROSO, Luis Roberto. **The Control of Constitutionality in Brazilian Law.** Sao Paulo: Saraiva, 2012. p. 23 to 32. [3] BARROSO, Luis Roberto. **The Control of Constitutionality in Brazilian Law.** Sao Paulo: Saraiva, 2012. p. 23 to 32.

on the basis of a 1789 law *(the Judiciary Act),* which had given the Supreme Court original jurisdiction to hear and determine cases of this nature. The Court designated the 1802 session to hear the case.

However, Congress repealed the law reorganizing the federal judiciary, abolishing the positions that had been created and dismissing their occupants. This situation was aggravated by two moments of tension: a) Thomas Jefferson did not consider any court decision ordering the government to hand over the investiture acts to be legitimate, and signaled that he would not comply with it; b) at the beginning of 1802, the House launched impeachment proceedings against a Federalist judge, in a political standoff that threatened to extend to the Justices of the Supreme Court.

It was in this politically hostile environment that the Supreme Court convened in 1803 to rule on Marbury v. Madison, which was the first decision in which the Court asserted its power to exercise constitutionality control, denying application to laws that, according to its interpretation, were unconstitutional.

Marbury v. Madison, therefore, was the decision that inaugurated the control of constitutionality in modern constitutionalism, establishing the principle of the supremacy of the constitution, the subordination to it of all state powers and the jurisdiction of the judiciary as its final interpreter, with the power to invalidate acts that contravene it.[4]

2.2 COLLECTIVE ACTIONS IN BRAZILIAN LAW

Law 7.347, of 24.07.1985, the Public Civil Action Law, was not the first to provide procedural mechanisms for defending diffuse interests, since twenty years ago the country's legal system already had Law 4.717, of 29.06.1965, regulating popular action, and since 1981 Law 6.938 had already provided in its art. The LACP was undoubtedly the greatest milestone in collective legal

---

[4] BARROSO, Luis Roberto. **The Control of Constitutionality in Brazilian Law.** Sao Paulo: Saraiva, 2012. p. 23 to 32.

protection in Brazil as it is known today, anticipating the advances that would later materialize in the 1988 Federal Constitution and the Consumer Protection Code.

Its importance stems, firstly, from the incorporation into the Brazilian legal system of the most advanced European legislative experiences and doctrinal studies, especially from Italy, France and Germany, as well as the North American experience on access to justice for collective rights: the legitimacy of associations, as well as the possibility of the public sector acting in defense of collective rights in the broadest sense, a review of the limits of res judicata and the provision of new and innovative powers to the magistrate, especially with regard to the mandamus effect of decisions (to do and not to do), much broader than the mere annulment of the harmful act provided for in the popular action law. Also because the law was able to adapt European and North American doctrine and experience to the Brazilian reality, specifically with regard to the role of the Public Prosecutor's Office, which already stood out in our country as an important defender of the environment, a role that in Europe, whose civil society has historically been more organized and combative than ours, was played almost exclusively by civil associations and in the United States by the individual who qualified as a suitable representative of the category and proved it. It was also because the law came into being with the intention - only consolidated with the consumer protection code in 1990 - of protecting all collective interests, a circumstance that to this day puts Brazilian law at the forefront internationally.[5]

The LACP, although it provided for significant advances, such as the legitimacy of civil associations, the possibility of granting a court order determining compliance with a requirement to do or not do something, and the granting of an injunction, as well as the establishment of a fund to which the compensation obtained in court should be directed, the resources of which would revert to the reconstruction of damaged property and the waiver of advance payment of costs, expert salaries and other expenses, however, the text still

---

[5] MIRALE, Edis. **Public civil action after 20 years: effectiveness and challenges.** Sao Paulo: Revista dos Tribunais, 2005. p. 24 and 25.

deserved improvement.

It should be noted that it was more concerned with guaranteeing and regulating the legitimacy of associations to protect the environment, improving Law 6.938/1981, than ensuring effective judicial protection of diffuse rights as a whole. In general terms, it followed European doctrine, especially Italian and French doctrine, which tended to treat each type of collective right in isolation and was somewhat opposed to the legitimacy of the Public Prosecutor's Office.[6]

Based on the Bierrenbach project, the members of the Sao Paulo Public Prosecutor's Office drew up a new draft which, while maintaining the advances of the previous one, added: the applicability of the public civil action for the defense of consumers and any other diffuse interest; the functional jurisdiction of the location of the damage, the provision of a civil inquiry under the chairmanship of the Public Prosecutor's Office as an instrument of instruction prior to the filing of the action, dispensing with or speeding up the latter; the possibility of a precautionary measure to defend the same rights; the classification of the crime of refusing, delaying or omitting technical data that is essential to the filing of a public civil action and the very terminology of the action, clearly influenced by institutional legislation. It can be seen that these were important changes to guarantee the effectiveness and viability of the public civil action, as well as the necessary scope that was expected of it in order to enable the adequate collective jurisdictional protection that the Brazilian reality demanded.

The latter bill was presented to Justice Minister Ibrahim Abi-Ackel by the then president of the National Confederation of the Public Prosecutor's Office (Conanp), Luis Antonio Fleury Filho, and was endorsed by him. It was then presented as a message from the executive branch, signed by President Joao Figueiredo and sent to Congress on 23.02.1985, receiving in the Chamber No. 4.984/1985 and in the Senate, 20/1985. Due to the priority given to executive branch bills, this bill was considered and approved before the Bierrenbach Bill,

---

[6] MIRALE, Edis. **Public civil action after 20 years: effectiveness and challenges.** Sao Paulo: Revista dos Tribunais, 2005. p. 26 to 28.

and went on to receive presidential approval without any significant changes. However, the bill was not fully sanctioned. President Jose Sarney vetoed item IV of article 1, a provision that guaranteed the law's application to any other diffuse interest, and did the same with articles 4 and 5, II, where the expression was present. It thus restricted the law's applicability to the diffuse rights expressly provided for in sections I to III, i.e. the environment, the consumer and goods and rights of artistic, aesthetic, historical, tourist and landscape value

A great opportunity to provide broad protection for collective rights was lost. The reasons expressed in the veto as "public interest" were based on legal uncertainty, to the detriment of the common good, which arises from the very broad and imprecise scope of the expression "any other diffuse interest".

Although regrettable, the veto sent an important message to scholars interested in supporting the drafting of legislation: the lack of definition of the scope of the term diffuse interests and the etymological breadth it encompasses aroused particular fear. It was necessary to provide a legal definition, and this is what Law 8.078/1990, the Consumer Protection Code, did.[7] Furthermore, this definition is of particular relevance, and will be the basis of the next chapter.

It should be noted that the public civil action has established itself as a constitutional action designed to protect diffuse, collective and individual homogenous rights. Today, on Brazilian soil, this action is mostly regulated by Law 7.347/85 (LACP) and also by Title III of Law 8.078/90 (CDC), more specifically in its articles 81 to 100, 103 and 104.

3- PUBLIC CIVIL ACTION

3.1 - COLLECTIVE, DIFFUSE AND INDIVIDUAL HOMOGENEOUS RIGHTS

First of all, with regard to the question of terminology, a large part of the doctrine and case law state that the terms "public civil action" and "collective action" are synonymous. However, it is possible to make a procedural distinction, based on a material distinction made by the legislator himself.

Until the advent of the Consumer Protection Code, we only spoke of collective rights in the broad sense, encompassing both collective and diffuse rights. The CDC, in its article 81, sole paragraph and subsections, defines and distinguishes three types of what are called trans-individual rights (or meta-individual rights or collective rights in the broad sense): diffuse rights (subsection I), collective rights (subsection II) and homogeneous individual rights (subsection III) .[78910]

In the same law, in article 91, the legislator states that collective action is the appropriate instrument for the protection of homogeneous individual rights, making it clear that nowadays the expression "public civil action" should be used for the protection of diffuse and collective rights (article 81, p. u, items I and II of the CDC), and the term "collective action" for the defense of homogeneous individual rights (item III)[9].

---

[7] The defense of the interests and rights of consumers and victims may be exercised in court individually or collectively.
Sole paragraph. Collective defense will be exercised when it comes to:
I - diffuse interests or rights, understood, for the purposes of this code, as transindividual interests or rights, of an indivisible nature, owned by indeterminate persons linked by circumstances of fact;
10- collective interests or rights, understood for the purposes of this code as transindividual interests or rights of an indivisible nature held by a group, category or class of people linked to each other or to the opposing party by a basic legal relationship;
III - homogeneous individual interests or rights, understood as those arising from a common origin.

3.2 - APPLICABLE LEGISLATION

Public civil action is the name given by Law 7.347, of 1985, to the special procedure it established to promote the protection of trans-individual rights and interests. It is made up of a set of mechanisms designed to provide preventive, restorative and precautionary demands for any diffuse and collective rights and interests, namely "liability claims for moral and patrimonial damages" caused to the environment, the consumer, the urban order, goods and rights of artistic, aesthetic, historical, tourist and landscape value, the economic order and the popular economy and other diffuse and collective rights or interests (art. 1).

Since then, some variants of public civil actions have been instituted, such as: law 7.853, of 24.10.1989, whose articles 3 and 7 regulate the protection of the collective and diffuse rights and interests of people with disabilities; law 8.069, of 13.07.1990 (Statute of Children and Adolescents), whose articles 208 to 224 regulate the protection of the collective and diffuse rights and interests of children and adolescents; law 8.078, of 11.09.1990 (Consumer Protection Code), whose articles 208 to 224 regulate the protection of the collective and diffuse rights and interests of children and adolescents. 208 to 224 regulate the protection of the collective and diffuse rights and interests of children and adolescents; by Law 8.078, of 11.09.1990 (Consumer Defense Code), whose articles 81 to 104 (except for the part specifically related to homogenous individual rights, articles 91 to 100) regulate the protection of the rights and interests[11] diffuse and collective of consumers; by Law 10.741, of 1.10.2003 (Statute of the Elderly), which, in its articles 69 and 92, provides procedural rules for the protection of the rights and interests of people with disabilities. and 92, provide specific procedural rules for the protection of the collective and individual rights of the elderly.

Despite the variety, the above-mentioned actions have essentially maintained the procedural line adopted in Law 7.347 of 1985, which applies subsidiarily to all the others, and it is therefore appropriate to give them the

[11]ZAVASCKI, Teori Albino. **Processo Coletivo - Tutela de Direitos Coletivos e Tutela Coletiva de Direitos.** São Paulo: Revista dos Tribunais, 2011. p.53 and 54.

common name of public civil action.

3.3 - OBJECT

The public civil action is a procedure tailored to the nature of the rights and interests it is intended to protect: transindividual rights (diffuse and collective). The variety and breadth of the claims that can be brought under it can be identified by a systematic examination of the aforementioned normative provisions, especially those of Law No. 7.347/85, and special care must be taken to avoid isolated and literal interpretations of its provisions.

According to Article 1 of this law, the public civil action is a means of pursuing claims arising from liability for moral and property damage caused to the environment, the consumer, goods and rights of artistic, aesthetic, historical, tourist and landscape value, infringement of the economic order and popular economy, the urban order and, in general, any other diffuse and collective interest.

Although it is called a precautionary measure, the action aimed at preventing damage to a material right is obviously aimed at obtaining preventive protection. It is not, therefore, a matter of precautionary protection (=provisional, formed on the basis of judgments of verisimilitude, to guarantee the usefulness of the process, subject to modification or revocation), but of definitive protection (albeit preventive) of the material right itself (= protection formed on the basis of exhaustive cognition, capable of forming res judicata).

It is clear that the public civil action is a multi-purpose instrument, which makes it an efficient means of providing full protection for trans-individual rights: preventive and reparatory protection, to obtain pecuniary (compensation in money) or personal (to fulfill obligations to do and not to do).

As far as the object of the public civil action is concerned, according to Luis Roberto Barroso, there is indeed a specific part and a claim brought before the courts, by means of a request, which is in no way to be confused with a declaration of unconstitutionality. The immediate object of the claim is the judicial measure requested. The mediate object of the claim is the good that the plaintiff intends to obtain by means of that measure.

3.4 - ACTIVE LEGITIMACY

D Article 5 of Law 7.347/85, as amended by Law 11.448/07 that the following have legal standing to bring the main action and the precautionary action: the Public Prosecutor's Office, the Public Defender's Office, the Union, the States, the Federal District and the Municipalities, an autarchy, a public company, a foundation or a mixed-capital company, associations which, at the same time, have been established for at least one (1) year under the terms of civil law, which include, among their institutional purposes, the protection of the environment, the consumer, the economic order, free competition or artistic, aesthetic, historical, tourist and landscape heritage.

As for the legitimacy of the Public Defender's Office and the public law bodies referred to in the Public Civil Action Law (Union, States, Federal District, Municipalities), , active legitimacy must necessarily be linked to an interest in acting. According to art. 3 of the CPC and n it is necessary to have an interest and legitimacy to bring or contest the action. Although not expressly mentioned in the normative text, there is an implicit condition of legitimacy in relation to them: not just any public civil action can be brought by such entities, but only those aimed at protecting trans-individual rights that are in some way related to the plaintiff's interests. Whether because of its activities, its powers, its assets or its services, or for any other reason, it is essential to be able to identify a pertinent relationship between the request made by the entity bringing the public civil action and its own interests and objectives as an institution.

It should also be noted that with regard to the legitimacy of the Public

Defender's Office, there is the natural limitation arising from its institutional functions which, according to art. 134 of the Constitution, are legal advice and the defense, at all levels, of the needy, in the form of art. 5, LXXIV. This means that the public civil actions that can be brought by it are restricted to those in which the assets to be protected concern the interests of people who are known to lack financial resources.

And he same relationship of interest must be present when the claim is brought by the other parties entitled under Article 5 of Law 7.347/85, namely, municipalities, public companies, foundations, mixed-capital companies and associations. In order for any of them to have the right to sue, there must also be evidence of an advantage, even if only in a general sense, for their own interests, if the claim is successful. With regard to associations, there are also the limits of points *a* and *b of* item V, the first of which reserves active legitimacy to associations with a certain stability (one year of existence), which discourages possible excesses or abuses in the filing of public civil actions; and the second, more directly linked to the interest in acting, imposes I an objective link, expressed in the statutes, between the claim made in the action and the institutional purposes of the action.[12]

3.4.1 - Legitimacy of the Public Prosecutor's Office

The Constitution of the Republic only provides for the legitimacy of the Public Prosecutor's Office to defend diffuse and collective rights[13] , but in 1990, with the advent of the Consumer Defense Code, there was express provision for the collective protection of homogeneous individual rights[14] , which are not

12 ZAVASCKI, Teori Albino. Processo Coletivo - Tutela de Direitos Coletivos e Tutela Coletiva de Direitos. Sao Paulo: Revista dos Tribunais, 2011. p.62 and 63.
13 Art. 129 of the Constitution: "The Public Ministry's institutional functions are: III - to promote civil investigations and public civil actions to protect public and social assets, the environment and other diffuse and collective interests; (...)".
14Art. 81 of the CDC: "The defense of the interests and rights of consumers and victims may be exercised in court individually or collectively. Single paragraph. Collective defense will be exercised when it concerns: III - homogeneous individual interests or rights, understood as

essentially collective, but which allow for collective treatment due to damage of common origin.

The question then arose as to whether the Public Prosecutor's Office could only act, under the terms of the constitutional provision, as an active party for the protection of diffuse and collective rights, or whether, under the terms of the subsequent provision of the Consumer Protection Code , it could also act to protect homogeneous individual rights.

On the issue, Luiz Paulo Araujo Filho[15] clarifies the controversy well, explaining the following: (...) two basic solutions seem admissible, and have been put forward by the Superior Court of Justice: a restrictive one, based on art. 25, item IV, letter "a", of Law no. 8.625/93, recognizing the legitimacy of the Public Prosecutor's Office exclusively for actions relating to unavailable homogeneous individual interests; another, in our view more appropriate to the constitutional system and therefore preferable, which accepts the legitimacy of the Public Prosecutor's Office for collective actions relating to unavailable individual rights, provided that the matter is of social interest.

Nowadays, the predominant question is whether or not the homogeneous individual interests dealt with collectively are of the necessary magnitude to characterize a genuine social interest, so as to legitimize the Public Prosecutor's Office to bring the action.

As a general rule, the proportion of homogeneous individual rights, the importance of the legal issue at stake, the condition of the people affected and the social dimension end up making homogeneous individual rights not simply individual rights, but real social interests, which consequently gives the Public Prosecutor's Office legitimacy to protect them.

---

those arising from a common origin."

[15] ARAUJO FILHO, Luiz Paulo da Silva. **Apoes colectivas: a tutela jurisdicional dos direitos individuais homogeneos**. 1. ed. Rio de Janeiro: Forense, 2000, p. 193.

3.5 - JUDGMENT AND RES JUDICATA

In a public civil action, the granting of the claim will mean, depending on the case, the granting of general or specific, liquid or illiquid, condemnatory, declaratory, constitutive, mandamus or executive judicial protection, by means of a sentence that is congruent with the nature of the claim. And, as already mentioned, the public civil action allows for injunctions of any kind . In the case of an obligation to do something, or not to do something or to deliver something, the sentence will be enforceable *latu sensu,* in the form of articles 461 and 461-A of the CPC. This means that it will be enforced within the same procedural relationship in which it was handed down, and not in an independent enforcement action.

The nature of the judgment in a public civil action is another important difference to be noted in relation to what happens in collective actions for the protection of homogeneous individual rights. In collective actions, as will be seen, the judgment has a peculiar nature, since it only grants protection with a generic content, with a judgment limited to the scope of the homogeneity of the rights which are the subject of the claim, leaving it up to another judgment to decide on the individual and heterogeneous situations relating to each injured party. In the case of a public civil action, the judgment will make a broad and specific judgment, as complete as possible, on the controversy. According to Victor Fairen Guillen, this is a "plenary claim".[16] The strict rule of the caput of art. 286 of the CPC applies to it, according to which the request must be certain and not generic, which will result, by the principle of congruence (CPC, art. 460), in a judgment with a similar character.

Article 16 of Law 7.437/85 establishes that, in a public civil action, the judgment "shall be res judicata *erga omnes*, within the limits of the territorial jurisdiction of the issuing body, except if the claim is dismissed for insufficient evidence, in which case any legitimate party may bring another action on the

---

[16] GUILLEN, Victor Fairen. El juicio ordinario y los plenarios rapidos, p. 53.

same grounds, using new evidence". Material res judicata, as defined in art. 467 of the CPC, is understood to be "the effectiveness which renders a judgment immutable and indisputable and no longer subject to ordinary or extraordinary appeal". Res judicata, therefore, is a phenomenon that takes place exclusively at the level of law. It is a quality of the judgment: its immutability. Before and after res judicata, the content of the judgment does not change. It remains exactly the same. What is added, with res judicata, is only its condition that it can no longer be reformed or annulled by appeal.

3.5.1 - Art. 16 of the Public Civil Action Act

With regard to the scope of effectiveness, the immutability of a judgment in a public civil action, according to article 16 of Law 7.347/85, "is *erga omnes*, within the limits of the territorial jurisdiction of the issuing body". The universal subjective extension *(erga omnes)* is a natural consequence of the transindividuality and indivisibility of the right protected in the action. If the rights being protected are indivisible and belong to a collectivity, to undetermined subjects, there is no way to establish subjective limits to the immutability of the judgment. Either it is immutable, and therefore will be for everyone, or it is not mutable, and therefore does not become res judicata. On the other hand, the *erga omnes* clause certainly does not go so far as to jeopardize the legal situation of third parties. Also applicable to res judicata in public civil actions is the limitation contained in article 472 of the CPC, which reads as follows: although third parties may benefit, they can never be negatively affected by a judgment handed down in a case in which they were not a party.

In the article in question, there is a second limitation on res judicata: the "limits of the territorial jurisdiction of the adjudicating body". A literal interpretation of the provision suggests that res judicata would be limited to a specific physical space. It would be difficult to reconcile this kind of limitation with the legal nature of res judicata (which is nothing more than a quality of the judgment, its immutability). What becomes res judicata (i.e. what becomes immutable) in judgments on the merits is the judgment contained therein regarding the existence or non-existence or way of being of the legal relationship which is the subject of the litigation, and this is no different in public civil actions. Although the holders of the right under protection are indeterminate, in these actions the cognitive activity also aims to obtain a judgment with a declaration of certainty regarding a specific legal relationship, born of a specific factual situation, which generates, or may generate, damage to a right, transindividual (belonging to a collectivity or to indeterminate subjects). It is this judgment of certainty that, through the effect of res judicata, becomes immutable. It is incomprehensible how the immutability thus constituted can be territorially divided, being limited, for example, to a district or a city. On the other hand. Considering that res judicata does not alter the content of the judgment, nor does it compromise its effectiveness, any limitation would mean, in practice, the production of a strange judgment, with two qualities: it would be valid, effective and immutable in a given territory, but it would be valid, effective and mutable outside that territory.

The literal interpretation of art. 16 therefore leads to a result that is incompatible with the institute of res judicata. There is no way of territorially dividing the quality of the judgment or the legal relationship certified in it. It should be noted that, in the case of transindividual rights, the disputed legal relationship, although with an indeterminate plurality of subjects in its active pole, is one and the same (indivisible). As such, the territorial limitation of res judicata is, in practice, ineffective in relation to it. A judgment of certainty about the existence or non-existence or mode of being of a legal relationship (which is a phenomenon of the world of thoughts) cannot be territorially circumscribed (a circumstance of the physical world).[17]

However, at the end of 2011, res judicata began to be treated more appropriately by the Superior Court of Justice, following the judgment in REsp

---

[17] ZAVASCKI, Teori Albino. Processo Coletivo - Tutela de Direitos Coletivos e Tutela Coletiva de Direitos. Sao Paulo: Revista dos Tribunais, 2011.

No. 1.243.887, when the teratological limitation on the effects of res judicata provided for in Article 16 of Law No. 7.347/85 (Public Civil Action Law) was removed. The Superior Court of Justice recognized that res judicata in public civil actions has nationwide effects.

It is true that the Special Court of the Superior Court of Justice, in December 2012, announced that it had ruled again on the issue, in EREsp No. 1.243.386, in order to decide the divergent judgments, which applied art. 16 of the Public Civil Action Law and REsp No. 1.243.887, but the idea is already beginning to spread that there should be no limitation on the effects of res judicata.

4 - CONTROL OF CONSTITUTIONALITY

4.1 - CONSTITUTIONAL SUPREMACY AND CONSTITUTIONALITY CONTROL

The legal system, as we know, is a hierarchical system of rules at the top of which is the Constitution. Constitutional norms are those created by the original or reforming constituent power and will normally be integrated into a written and rigid Constitution. The norms that appear in the formal Constitution of the State are endowed with supremacy, enjoying legal superiority over the other norms in the system. Infra-constitutional norms are all the norms of the legal order, issued by the constituted powers, and which do not enjoy constitutional stature. Infra-constitutional norms are called primary when they have their basis of validity directly in the constitution and are capable of innovating in the legal order; and secondary when they are intended to regulate or specify aspects of the law (in a broad sense, this includes the constitution itself and primary norms) .[18]

It should be noted that the main characteristic of constitutional norms is their position in the system, where they enjoy legal superiority over all other norms. Constitutional supremacy is the postulate on which all contemporary constitutionalism is based. It follows that no law, no normative act, strictly speaking, no legal act, can subsist validly if it is incompatible with the Constitution.

And to ensure this supremacy, the control of the constitutionality of laws was created, enshrined since the swift case of Marbury v. Madison, judged by the US Supreme Court in 1803, without prejudice to remote antecedents.[19] Interpretation in accordance with the Constitution, which subordinates the

---

[18] BARROSO, Luis Roberto. **Course in contemporary constitutional law.** Sao Paulo: Saraiva, 2010. p. 191.
[19] CAPPELLETTI, Mauro. **Judicial control of the constitutionality of laws in comparative law.** 1999, p.45 and s.

meaning of infra-constitutional norms to constitutional principles and rules, also pays homage to supremacy.[20] The constitutional norm, therefore, is the parameter of validity and the interpretative reference point for all the norms in the legal system.

In Brazil, where the control of constitutionality is eminently judicial in nature - that is, it is up to the organs of the judiciary to have the final say on the constitutionality or otherwise of a rule - there are, however, various instances of political control of constitutionality, both within the executive branch - e.g. the veto of a bill on the grounds of unconstitutionality - and within the legislative branch - e.g. the rejection of a bill by the Constitutionality and Justice Commission of the legislative house on the grounds of unconstitutionality, the veto of a law on the grounds of unconstitutionality, - and in the Legislative Branch - e.g. the rejection of a bill by the Constitutionality and Justice Committee of the legislative house on the grounds of unconstitutionality.[21]

As for the system of control exercised by the judiciary, Brazil follows a very peculiar model, characterized by the fact that it is an eclectic control, since it is processed in two ways: diffuse (by incidental means) and concentrated (by main or direct action). These two mechanisms form the Brazilian system of constitutionality control, which is a mixture of the control systems adopted in the United States and Austria.[22]

4.1.1 - Assumptions

The exercise of constitutionality control requires the fulfillment of certain presuppositions, some of which are inescapable, others which are subject to exceptions.

The first prerequisite would be the existence of a rigid Constitution, i.e. a

[20] MENDES, Gilmar Ferreira. **Jurisdipao constitucional,** 2005, p. 287-295 and 346-356.
[21] BARROSO, Luis Roberto. **The control of constitutionality in Brazilian law**, 2012, p.66.
[22] BARROSO, Luis Roberto. **Fundamental concepts on the control of constitutionality and tho jurisprudence of the Federal Supreme Court**, p. 233 to 268.

Charter that has a more solemn and difficult legislative process for its amendment.[23]

The second presupposition is constitutional supremacy, which for many comes from rigidity itself. Despite this respectable position, we disagree with the idea that supremacy is generated by rigidity.

The supremacy of the Political Charter is essential for the control of constitutionality, but it is believed that supremacy does not occur because of the way in which it is modified (constitutional rigidity), but because of the basis of its validity. The Constitution of the Republic is the top rung of the normative hierarchy, all the rules of the national legal system have their basis of validity, whether immediate or indirect, in the Mother Law. If the apex of the normative hierarchy is the Political Charter and the higher norm is the basis of validity of the immediately lower norm,[24] the Constitution is supreme in relation to the other norms.

The third and final prerequisite is the existence of a control body, an interpreter who ensures that constitutional precepts are respected.

In Brazil, the "filter" is the Supreme Court, when the issue is the Constitution of the Republic, and the State Court of Justice, when the parameter is the State Constitution. However, it should not be forgotten that there is diffuse control, which allows all bodies to exercise constitutionality control.[22] [25]

4.1.2 - Constitutionality bloc

In Brazil, the constitutionality bloc can be understood as the set of rules, principles, constitutional values, provisions of the Transitional Provisions Acts (ADCT), Constitutional Amendments and International Treaties with constitutional hierarchy (art. 5, p.3, CRFB), which serve as a parameter for the control of

---

[23] LENZA, Pedro. Op. Cit. P. 117; PAULO, Vicente and ALEXANDRINO, Marcelo. **Control of Constitutionality.** 4 ed. Rio de Janeiro: Impetus, 2006. p. 5.

[24] KELSEN, Hans. **Pure Theory of Law**. 2. Ed. Sao Paulo: Martins Fontes. 1939. P. 138.

[25] PADILHA, Rodrigo. **Systematized Constitutional Law.** 2ªed. Rio de Janeiro: Forense, 2012.

constitutionality.[26]

The concept of the constitutionality bloc is an intermediary one, since it is more restricted and the normative hierarchy is essential to serve as a parameter for the control of constitutionality.

By making use of the constitutionality bloc, the control parameter grows too much insofar as, in addition to everything that has been said, there are provisions of Constitutional Amendments that are not incorporated into the text of the constitution because they have a transitional nature, but which can be used as a parameter for controlling constitutionality because the legal nature of the constitutional amendment is that of a constitutional norm.

4.2 - TYPES OF UNCONSTITUTIONALITY

The unconstitutionality of a norm or normative act can be assessed on the basis of different elements or criteria, including the moment in which it occurs, the type of state action that caused it, the procedure for drafting it and the content of the norm, among others. The following types of unconstitutionality should be highlighted: formal and material, by action and by omission.

The first possibility to consider with regard to the defect of form is what is known as *organic* constitutionality, which is the failure to comply with the rule of competence for issuing the act.

If, for example, the Legislative Assembly of a Federal State enacts a law on criminal matters[2427] or on civil law[28] , it incurs unconstitutionality by violating

---

[26] PADILHA, Rodrigo. **Systematized Constitutional Law**. 2ªed. Rio de Janeiro: Forense, 2012.

[27] STF, RDA, 186:148, 1991, ADIn 403-BA, rel. Min. Marco Aurelio: it is unconstitutional for a state constitution to legalize the operation of casinos in its territory, as this is a criminal matter, which falls within the exclusive competence of the Union. STF, DJU, Sept. 1, 2000, ADInMC 1.901-MG, rel. Min. Ilmar Galvao: State Constitution cannot create a hypothesis of a crime of responsibility.

[28] STF, *inf. STF, 133:1,* Nov. 1998, ADInMC 1.918-ES, rel. Min. Mauricio Correa: state law cannot prohibit the charging of parking fees by private establishments, as it is formally unconstitutional, violating the Federal Union's exclusive competence to legislate on civil law.

the Union's competence in the matter[29] . On the other hand, there will be *formal* unconstitutionality per se if a certain type of law is produced without observing the proper legislative process.

With regard to material unconstitutionality, it expresses a substantive incompatibility between the law or normative act and the Constitution. It can be expressed as a confrontation with a constitutional rule - e.g., the setting of the reappointment of a category of public servants above the constitutional limit (art. 37, XI, CR) - or with a constitutional principle, as in the case of a law that illegitimately restricts the participation of candidates in public examinations on the grounds of gender and age (arts. 5, *caput*, and 3, IV), in disharmony with the commandment of isonomy. The material control of isonomy can be based on all categories of constitutional norms: organizational, rights-defining and programmatic .[30]

There are other ways in which unconstitutionality can occur: it is possible to violate the Constitution by carrying out an act that it prohibited or by failing to carry out an act that it required. Because this is the case, the Constitution can be violated through action, positive conduct, or through omission, illegitimate inaction. [31]

4.3 - DIFFUSE CONTROL

The incidental control of constitutionality is exercised in a diffuse manner, and is the responsibility of all judicial bodies without distinction, both at first and second level, as well as the higher courts. As it is an inherent part of the normal performance of the judicial function, any judge or court, in the act of realizing the Law in the concrete situations submitted to them, has the power and duty to stop

---

[29] Federal Constitution: it is the exclusive competence of the Union to legislate on criminal law and civil law (art. 22, I), a competence it exercises through the National Congress (art. 48).

[30] On the classification of constitutional norms, see Luis Roberto Barroso, *O direito constitucional e a efetividade de suas normas,* 2003.

[31] BARROSO, Luis Roberto. **The control of constitutionality in Brazilian law.** 2012, p. 53.

applying the legislative act that conflicts with the Constitution.

Singularly, the power of the monocratic judge of the first degree to deny application to a rule that he considers unconstitutional is exercised more fully and simply than the power of the courts to take the same action. And for the incidental declaration of unconstitutionality[32] , the courts are subject to the principle of *plenary reservation* (CF, art. 97)[33] - with fractional bodies, such as chambers or panels, being prohibited from declaring unconstitutionality - and to a specific procedure established by the Code of Civil Procedure (arts. 480 to 482), to which the 2nd degree courts (State Courts of Justice, in the case of state justice, and Federal Regional Courts, in the case of common federal justice) and the higher courts, including the Superior Court of Justice(31).[34]

In fact, the first characteristic of this type of control, according to Luis Roberto Barroso, is the need for a dispute to be brought before the courts. And by deciding the dispute, the constitutional question is decided incidentally, since the object of the action is not the constitutionality or otherwise of the normative act, but only a question that is essential to the judgment on the merits .[35]

Diffuse control is mainly characterized by the fact that it can only be exercised in a concrete case to be decided by the Judiciary. Thus, once a dispute has been brought to court, the Judiciary must resolve it and to do so, incidentally, it must analyze the constitutionality or otherwise of the normative act. The declaration of unconstitutionality is necessary for the outcome of the specific case, and is therefore not the main object of the action .[36]

4.3.1 - The principle of plenary reserve

[32] Lenio Luiz Streck, *Jurisdicao constituucional e hermen6utica.* 2002, p. 362-3.

[33] This is what CF 88 states: "Art. 97: Only by a vote of the absolute majority of its members or of the members of the respective special body may the courts declare a law or normative act of the Public Power to be unconstitutional".

[34] BARROSO, Luis Roberto. **The control of constitutionality in Brazilian law.** 2012, p. 118 and 119.

[35] BARROSO, Luis Roberto. **Fundamental concepts on the control of constitutionality and the jurisprudence of the Federal Supreme Court.** p.247.

[36] MORAES, Alexandre de. **Constitutional Law,** p. 562.

Article 97 of the 1988 Constitution of the Republic states that the Courts can only declare a state normative act unconstitutional by a vote of an absolute majority of its members or of the members of its special body. This principle applies to all courts, including the Supreme Court, when exercising concentrated control[3437] . It does not apply to declarations of constitutionality or to monocratic judges.

Articles. 480 and 482 of the Civil Procedure Code govern this rule. If the unconstitutionality of a law or normative act of a public authority is alleged, the rapporteur, after hearing the Public Prosecutor's Office, will submit the matter to the panel or chamber that has jurisdiction over the case. If the allegation is rejected, the trial shall continue; if it is upheld, a judgment shall be drawn up so that the matter may be submitted to the full court.

Making the plenary rule more flexible, Law No. 9.756/98 added a single paragraph to article 481 of the CPC, which reads as follows: "The fractional bodies of the courts shall not submit arguments of constitutionality to the plenary or special bodies when they or the plenary of the Supreme Court have already ruled on the matter."

However, if there is no such decision, they are obliged to submit it to the plenary or special body. In this sense, Binding Summula No. 10 states: "The decision of a fractional body of a court which, although it does not expressly declare the unconstitutionality of a law or normative act of the Public Authorities, removes its incidence in whole or in part, violates the clause of plenary reserve (art. 97 of the Constitution)". This means that the decision of the plenary or special body will be binding on the court where it is issued, as well as the decision of the STF plenary being binding on all courts. It should be noted, however, that first instance judges remain free to decide .[38]

4.3.2 - Effects of the decision

A decision that rules out the applicability of an unconstitutional law to a

[37] MORAES, Alexandre de. **Constitutional Law,** p. 562 and 563.
[38] RUSSO, Luciana. **Constitutional Law.** 2012, p. 59 and 60.

specific case does not lead to the annulment of the normative act, which remains fully valid in the legal system and can be applied in similar cases. According to Paulo Bonavides, a law that offends the constitution does not thus disappear from the legal order of the body or system of laws, and may still apply in another case, unless the competent power repeals it. So the judgment does not attack the law in theory or in the abstract, nor does it imply the formal annulment of its provisions, the application of which is only limited to the case in question. This is the so-called relativity of res judicata. There is nothing to prevent the law from being applied in other proceedings, in analogous cases, before the same judge or another judge .[39]

The effects of this decision benefit only the parties to the dispute and reach the unconstitutional normative act from its origin, which means that they are *inter partes* and *ex tunc* .[40]

This last effect is due to what Gilmar Ferreira Mendes considers to be an implicit constitutional principle, that of the nullity of an unconstitutional law. According to the Supreme Court's opinion, "recognizing the validity of an unconstitutional law - even for a limited time - would represent a break with the principle of the supremacy of the constitution .[41]

4.3.3 - The suspension by the Federal Senate

Once the Federal Supreme Court has declared a normative act unconstitutional, either on appeal or in its original jurisdiction, it is up to the STF to communicate the decision to the Federal Senate, so that the effects of art. 52, X of the Constitution can take effect, according to which it is up to the legislative body to "suspend the execution, in whole or in part, of a law declared unconstitutional by a final decision of the STF".

By doing so through a resolution, the Senate suspends the effectiveness

[39] BONAVIDES, Paulo. **Constitutional Law Course,** p. 273 and 274.
[40] *Ex Tunc* means "from then" or "since then; with retroactive effect". SILVIA , De Placito e. Vocabulo juridico, p. 329.
[41] MENDES, Gilmar Ferreira. **Jurisdigao Constitucional: o controle abstrato de normas no Brasilo na Alemanha.** 3rd Ed. Sao Paulo: Saraiva, 1999, p. 203 and 204.

of the law deemed unconstitutional by the STF, extending the effects of the declaration of unconstitutionality, which becomes *erga omnes* and *ex nunc*[42] , to everyone in the same situation. And since the Senate's suspensive resolution has merely *ex nunc effects,* those who want to be protected by the retroactive effects will have to go to court to have their rights fully protected, via the diffuse route .[43]

The act of the Senate that suspends the effectiveness of the unconstitutional rule is a discretionary act, which means that the legislative body is not obliged to issue it, but does so according to political criteria.

In the case of suspension of execution, the Federal Senate has a general competence and not a constitutionally determined duty to act. The Senate's competence consists of a discretionary activity of a political nature. The suspensive resolution is a political act that gives *erga omnes* effect to the Supreme Court's decision in a specific case. It is up to the Senate to examine the advisability and opportunity of considering, in theory, suspending the effects of removing a legal or regulatory provision from the legal system. It is not obliged to issue a suspensive resolution. Today it is taken for granted, and the polemic waged by the doctrine on the issue has therefore been practically exhausted, that the Senate is the exclusive judge of when it is appropriate to exercise the competence attributed to it, and only to it, to suspend a law or decree declared unconstitutional by a definitive decision of the STF .[44]

4.4 - CONCENTRATED CONTROL

The jurisdictional function, as a general rule, is designed to resolve conflicts of interest, to judge a dispute between parties who have antagonistic

---

[42] *Ex nunc* means "from now on; from the present moment, without retroactive effect". SILVIA, De Placdo e. **Vocabulario Juridico**, p. 329.
[43] AGRA, Walber de Moura. **Manual of Constitutional Law**, p. 520 and 421.
[44] CLEVE, Clemerson Merlin. **The abstract review of constitutionality in Brazilian law**, p. 121 to 122.

claims[45] . The control of constitutionality by direct action or by principal route, or even called concentrated control, although also jurisdictional, is an atypical exercise of jurisdiction, because in it there is no litigation or concrete situation to be resolved through the application of the law by the judging body. Its object is a pronouncement on the law itself. It is said that the control is in theory or abstract because there is no concrete case underlying the judicial manifestation. Direct action is aimed at protecting the legal system itself, avoiding the presence of an element that is not harmonious, incompatible with the constitution. It is an objective process, without parties, which does not lend itself to the protection of subjective rights, of individual legal situations. In the specific case of unconstitutionality by omission, the declaration is also in theory, in a pronouncement recognizing the illegitimate inertia of the body responsible for issuing the rule required by the legal system .[46]

Concentrated control of constitutionality has its origins in the Austrian model, which spread throughout Europe, and consists of assigning the guardianship of the Constitution to a single body or a limited number of them, instead of the American model of supervision by all the courts (diffuse system).

In the Brazilian case, the Constitution provides for the possibility of concentrated control, by principal means, to be carried out: at the federal level, and with the Constitution of the Republic as the paradigm, by the Superior Federal Court, in the direct action of unconstitutionality of a federal or state law or normative act, in the declaratory action of constitutionality of a federal law or act (art. 102, I, "*a*", CR) and in the action of unconstitutionality by omission (art. 103, p.2, CR); at the state level, the State Constitution is the paradigm, by the Court of Justice, in the representation of unconstitutionality of state or municipal laws or normative acts (art. 103, p.2, CR).At state level, the paradigm is the State Constitution, by the Court of Justice, in the representation of unconstitutionality of

[45] FAGUNDES, Seabra. **The control of administrative acts by the Judiciary,** 1979, p.11.
[46] BARROSO, Luis Roberto. **The control of constitutionality in Brazilian law.** 6ª Ed. Sao Paulo: Saraiva, 2012, p. 179 and 180.

state or municipal laws or normative acts (art. 125, p.2)[44 47]

4.4.1 - Direct action for unconstitutionality

The direct action of unconstitutionality or normative act, also known as a generic action, was introduced into Brazilian law by constitutional amendment no. 16, of November 26, 1965, to the 1946 Constitution, which referred to it as representation. The ADI procedure is regulated in Law 9.868/99 and in the STF's internal regulations, which are applied subsidiarily.

The ADI is an abstract control action, under the jurisdiction of the Federal Supreme Court, which aims to declare the unconstitutionality of a federal, state or district law or normative act in the exercise of state legislative powers. It performs, in a concentrated and, *ipso facto,* private manner, the abstract control of the constitutionality of norms in the face of the Charter of the Republic, in the hypotheses in which it is appropriate (art. 102, I, *a)*.[48]

Passive legitimacy in a direct action for unconstitutionality lies with the bodies or authorities responsible for the law or normative act that is the subject of the action, which will provide information to the rapporteur of the case. The actual defense of the contested rule, whether federal or state, falls to the Attorney General of the Union, who acts as a kind of trustee of the presumption of legality of acts emanating from the Public Power.[49] Private individuals can never be a party to this type of action.

The 1988 constitution removed the monopoly of the Attorney General, since previously only he had this legitimacy, and expanded the list of active legitimates for direct actions, set out in the nine sections of art. 103 of the CRFB

---

[47] BARROSO, Luis Roberto. **The control of constitutionality in Brazilian law.** 6th Ed. Sao Paulo: Saraiva, 2012, p. 182.

[48] CRFB, art. 102: "The Federal Supreme Court is primarily responsible for guarding the Constitution: I - process and judge, originally: a) the direct action of unconstitutionality of a federal or state law or normative act and the declaratory action of constitutionality of a federal law or normative act (...)".

[49] CRFB, art. 103, p.3: "When the Federal Supreme Court assesses the unconstitutionality, in theory, of a legal rule or normative act, it shall previously cite the Attorney General of the Union, who will defend the act or text being challenged."

.[50]

The jurisprudence of the STF requires that some of the legitimate parties have thematic relevance, i.e. demonstrate an interest in the law that is being challenged, a requirement that must be met by the special legitimate parties, which are the following: State and Federal District Governments; the Bureau of the Legislative Assembly and the Bureau of the Legislative Chamber of the Federal District; Trade Union Confederations and National Class Entities. In contrast to these, the others are called universal legitimates, from whom proof of thematic relevance is not required .[51]

The Constitution expressly provides for the possibility of a precautionary order in direct actions of unconstitutionality[52] . This is an exceptional measure, as the best doctrine teaches, in view of the presumption of validity of state acts, including normative ones.

This is an exceptional measure, since state acts enjoy a presumption, *juris tantum*, of legitimacy, or in the case of constitutionality. When examining the STF's case law, we can identify the following general requirements: a) the plausibility of the thesis *(fumus boni iuris);* b) emergency *(periculum in mora);* and the prevailing public interest and the guarantee of the decision's subsequent effectiveness as specific requirements.[53]

The granting of a precautionary measure suspends the effectiveness of the contested rule, with effects, as a rule, *ex nunc*, i.e. not retroactive. However, following the STF's settled position, Law 9.868/99, in p. 1 of art. 11, establishes that the STF may give retroactive effect to the decision, if it deems it necessary.

---

[50] CRFB: "The following may propose direct actions for unconstitutionality and direct actions for constitutionality:I) the President of the Republic; II) the Board of the Federal Senate; III) the Board of the Chamber of Deputies; IV) the Board of the Legislative Assembly or the Legislative Chamber of the Federal District; V) the Governor of the State or the Federal District; VI) the Attorney General of the Republic; VII) the Federal Council of the Brazilian Bar Association; VIII) a political party with representation in the National Congress; IX) a trade union confederation or class entity of national scope".

[51] CLEVE, Clemerson Merlin. **A fiscalizagao abstrata da constitucionalidade do direito brasileiro**. 2ªed. Sao Paulo: Revista dos Tribunais, 2000 p.161 to 162.

[52] CRFB, art. 102, I, *p*: the STF is originally responsible for processing and judging "requests for precautionary measures in direct actions of unconstitutionality".

[53] SCHAFER, Gilberto. **Civil Action and Control of Constitutionality**, p. 92.

and in the case of abstract control of norms, the precautionary measure, just like the decision on the merits, *has erga omnes* effect[54]

Pursuant to Article 5 of Law 9.868/99, when a direct action for unconstitutionality is filed, it is not permissible to withdraw the application.

According to the non-exhaustive list drawn up by Jose Adonis Callou de Araujo Sa, the following are subject to abstract control of constitutionality: i) constitutional amendments; ii) complementary and ordinary federal and state laws; iii) provisional measures and legislative decrees; iv) decrees and other acts of the Executive Branch that have normative force and are not merely regulatory; v) provisions of state constitutions; v) regulations and other resolutions of the Courts .[55]

On the other hand, normative sentences issued by the Labor Court and collective bargaining agreements are not the object of direct action, even though they have normative content. This is because the former are judicial acts that can be challenged through the appropriate remedies, while collective agreements are not issued by the public authorities. Normative acts prior to the 1988 Constitution are also not subject to abstract control of norms, as the Supreme Court considers that in this case there is no question of unconstitutionality, but of repeal; as well as regulations or normative acts that go beyond the parameters of the law, as this is a case of illegality and not unconstitutionality, according to the Supreme Court's opinion .[56]

4.4.1.1 - Effects of the decision

The direct action of unconstitutionality declares the rule null and void. In the technical sense, before the vitiated rule is declared unconstitutional, it will be invalid but effective. Only after it has been declared unconstitutional will the rule

---

[54] MORAES, Alexandre de. **Constitutional Law.** 7aed. Sao Paulo: Atlas, 2000, p. 589 to 590.
[55] SA, Jose Adonis Callou de Araujo. **Public Civil Action and Control of Constitutionality**. p.75.
[56] CLEVE, Clemerson Merlin. **A fiscalizapao abstrata da constitucionalidade do direito brasileiro**. 2ªed. Sao Paulo: Revista dos Tribunais, 2000 p.215 to 218.

be invalid and ineffective.

The effects of a declaration of unconstitutionality will be *erga omnes* and binding. It is binding on the other organs of the judiciary and on the direct and indirect public administration at federal, state and municipal level, in accordance with Article 102(2) of the CRFB[57] . This means that it does not bind the legislative power in its typical (legislative) function .[58]

The effects of an ADI decision are not binding on the Supreme Court. Thus, even if the Federal Supreme Court has dismissed the case (declaring it unconstitutional), it may at any time re-examine the matter and, if it has changed its mind (constitutional change), declare the unconstitutionality of the contested rule .[59]

The temporal effect will be *ex tunc,* with the possibility of modulation of the effects, according to art. 27 of law n. 9.868/99, where the STF may, by a two thirds majority of its members, restrict the effects of the decision or decide that it will only be effective as of its final and unappealable decision or another moment that may be set.

Therefore, the declaration of unconstitutionality also has a repristinatory effect. In this sense, a direct declaration makes previous legislation applicable if it exists, unless the STF expressly states otherwise.

Despite the doctrinal position that the repristinatory effect does not exist when there is modulation of effects, the majority view is that even if the STF

---

57 CRFB: "The Federal Supreme Court is primarily responsible for guarding the Constitution: The final decisions on the merits handed down by the Federal Supreme Court in direct actions of unconstitutionality and in actions of declaratory judgment of constitutionality shall be effective against all and shall have binding effect in relation to the other organs of the Judiciary and the direct and indirect public administration at federal, state and municipal level."

58 Rcl n. 2.617/MG. Rapporteur: Minister Cesar Peluso. DJ, 20.05.2005: "(...) the general effectiveness and binding effect of a decision handed down by the Federal Supreme Court, in a direct action for the constitutionality or unconstitutionality of a federal law or normative act, only affects the other organs of the Judiciary and all those of the Executive Branch, not the legislature, which can issue a new law with the same normative content, without offending the authority of that decision".

59 PADILHA, Rodrigo. **Direito Constitucional esquematizado**. 2ª Ed. Rio de Janeiro: Forense. p. 182.

establishes *ex nunc* effects, a repristinatory effect is possible, otherwise there would be no point in applying a repristinatory effect to the preliminary injunction decision, since in this case the effect is *ex nunc* .[60]

The principle of partiality applies to constitutionality control decisions handed down by the Supreme Court. This means that the Supreme Court can declare that a word in the text of the provision is unconstitutional, provided that it does not alter the meaning of the rule or that the provision has an autonomous existence without the deleted word .[61]

4.4.2 - Direct action for unconstitutionality by omission

Unconstitutional omissions can occur within the ambit of the three branches of government, through illegitimate inaction to adopt (i) normative, (ii) political-administrative or (iii) judicial measures. With regard to omissions of a political administrative nature, there are a variety of legal remedies, in particular the writ of mandamus and the public civil action. Judicial omissions, on the other hand, must be remedied through the system of appeals established by procedural law, and are remedied within the judiciary. For this reason, the constitutional treatment of unconstitutionality by omission refers to omissions of a normative nature[62] , which can be attributed to both the Legislative branch, for the issuing of primary norms, and the Executive branch, when it has to issue secondary acts of a general nature, such as regulations, instructions or resolutions.

Due to constitutional dirigisme and the large number of rules with limited

---

[60] Law n. 9.868/99 Art. 11, p.2º: "Once the precautionary measure has been granted, the Federal Supreme Court shall publish the operative part of the decision in a special section of the Official Gazette of the Union and the Official Gazette of the Union, within ten days, and shall request information from the authority from which the act originated, observing, where applicable, the procedure established in Section I of this Chapter: The granting of the precautionary measure shall make the previous legislation applicable, unless expressly stated otherwise."

[61] PADILHA, Rodrigo, Op. Cit., p. 183.

[62] STF, DJU, 14 Apr. 1989, ADI 19, rel. Min. Aldir Passinho: "The direct action for unconstitutionality by omission referred to in p. 2 of art. 103 of the new CF, is not to be proposed so that a certain administrative act is practiced in a concrete case, but rather aims to have a normative act issued that becomes necessary for the fulfillment of a constitutional precept that, without it, could not be applied".

effectiveness, which, for their complete effectiveness, depend on the action of the ordinary legislator, the Brazilian Constitution of 1988, in addition to creating the writ of injunction, sought inspiration from Lusitania to create the direct action for unconstitutionality by omission, also known as the action to suppress omission .[63]

The purpose of a direct action for unconstitutionality by omission is to notify the competent authority of a legislative delay in regulating a constitutional rule of limited effectiveness, an inertia that makes it impossible to exercise rights provided for in the Constitution.

The constitution sought to treat abstract constitutional jurisdiction as a unit, with only the request varying, which could be a declaration of unconstitutionality, constitutionality or unconstitutionality by omission. In all three cases, the jurisdiction rule is written in the same constitutional provision, namely art. 102, I, a of the CRFB/88 .[64]

The active legitimates and the procedure of the ADI by omission are the same as those of the direct action for unconstitutionality, except for the procedure in which it is incompatible[65] . One of the differences between ADI's for omissions and ADI's for omissions is that a precautionary measure is not appropriate in the latter, according to the Supreme Court's understanding that, in this case, not even the ultimate judicial provision can imply the removal of the omission[66] . Another important difference concerns the effects of the decision, which will be clarified in the next section.

4.4.2.1 - Effects of the decision

The decision that judges the ADI for omission will be effective *erga omnes*

---

[63] PADILHA, Rodrigo. **Direito Constitucional esquematizado**. 2ª Ed. Rio de Janeiro: Forense. p. 192.

[64] BARROSO, Luis Roberto. **The control of constitutionality in Brazilian law.** 6ª Ed. Sao Paulo: Saraiva, 2012, p. 282.

[65] CLEVE, Clemerson Merlin. **A fiscalizapao abstrata da constitucionalidade do direito brasileiro**. 2aed. Sao Paulo: Revista dos Tribunais, 2000 p339.

[66]MORAES, Alexandre. **Constitutional Law.**

and *ex tunc,* whether or not it declares the omission unconstitutional. At this point, it should be emphasized that the omission will only be recognized as unconstitutional when the period of time in which the body responsible for the normative act has remained "silent" exceeds the limits of reasonableness .[67]

If the action is upheld, the STF will notify the administrative body responsible for issuing the act, which must do so within thirty days, under penalty of liability on the part of the Government, in which case the decision is of a mandamus nature. On the other hand, if the omission that was declared unconstitutional was by the Legislative Power, the STF will give notice to the National Congress to adopt the necessary measures, without, however, setting a deadline for doing so, in which case the decision is simply declaratory in nature. In the latter case, it will only be possible to speak of a mandamus effect when the omission results in damage, in which case the government will be liable for damages .[68]

4.4.2.2 - ADI for omissions and injunctions

Due to constitutional dirigisme and the large number of rules with limited effectiveness, which, for their complete effectiveness, depend on the action of the ordinary legislator, the Brazilian Constitution of 1988, in addition to creating the writ of mandamus, sought inspiration from Lusitania to create the direct action for unconstitutionality by omission, also known as an action to suppress omission.[69]

It is important to note that the writ of mandamus is provided for in Article 5, LXXI of the Federal Constitution of 1988, which states that this constitutional remedy will be granted whenever the lack of a regulatory rule makes it impossible to exercise constitutional rights and freedoms and the prerogatives inherent to nationality, sovereignty and citizenship.

---

[67] CLEVE, Clemerson Merlin. **A fiscalizapao abstrata da constitucionalidade do direito brasileiro**. 2aed. Sao Paulo: Revista dos Tribunais, 2000 p.346.
[68] AGRA, Walber de Moura. **Manual of Constitutional Law.** P. 512 and 513.
[69] PADILHA, Rodrigo. **Direito Constitucional sistematizado**. 2ª Ed. Rio de Janeiro: Ed. Forense. 2012. p. 192.

The writ of injunction differs from the ADI for omissions in that it is an instrument for controlling constitutionality that is carried out by means of a concrete fact. It is a legal instrument made available to any interested party who feels prevented from exercising a constitutionally guaranteed right due to the lack of a regulatory rule. The aim of the writ of mandamus is to ensure that the constitutional rule be applied in favor of the impetrant, regardless of regulation, it is precisely because it has not been regulated .[70]

However, with regard to the Direct Action for the Control of Constitutionality by Omission, it should be noted that this instrument of abstract control aims to suppress legislative inertia, that is, through its decision of a mandamus nature, the responsible body must adopt measures to make up for the absence of the regulatory norm, as provided for in art. 12-H, p. 1 of Law No. 9.868/99.

[70] SILVA, Jose Afonso da. **Course in positive constitutional law**. p. 452.

5. CONSTITUTIONALITY CONTROL IN PUBLIC CIVIL ACTION

5.1 - CRITICISM OF DIFFUSE CONTROL IN PUBLIC CIVIL ACTION

There is doctrinal resistance to the possibility of using diffuse control in a public civil action, as there are still those who argue that it is impossible to argue unconstitutionality in such an action, as it would usurp the jurisdiction of the Federal Supreme Court, to the extent that it would resemble the process established in a direct action for unconstitutionality. This is because the judgment handed down in a public civil action is *erga omnes*, which ends up generating, in practice, an effect of the abstract control of constitutionality .[71]

It is worth noting that in the case of judgments handed down in public civil actions, as provided for in Article 103 of the CDC, the judgment will have *erga omnes* effect when it refers to diffuse and homogeneous individual rights, in accordance with sections I and III, while in the case of collective rights the effects will be *ultra partes,* more limited to the group, category or class.

In this sense, it must be said that the concrete verification of this phenomenon is especially foreseeable in collective actions when, considering the terms of the claim, all the possible recipients of the rule whose unconstitutionality is the basis of the claim are included as defendants in the process. In situations like this, even if there has been no explicit request for a declaration of invalidity of the rule in the abstract, the judgment of upholding ends up having, in practice, the same universal effectiveness as the judgment in the concentrated control, since, transversely, it removes from the questioned rule all its potential for application, which is entirely exhausted, including for the future .[72]

---

[71] PADILHA, Rodrigo. **Direito constitucional sistematizado**. 2ª Ed. Rio de Janeiro: Editora Forense, 2012, p.151.

[72] ZAVASCKI, Teori Albino. **Processo Coletivo - Tutela de Direitos Coletivos e Tutela**

It is true that this would be the case, for example, in a case brought by the Public Prosecutor's Office against the Union, requesting that the defendant refrain from levying a certain tax, on the grounds that the law that created it is unconstitutional. Although unconstitutionality is the basis of the claim (in the cause of action), the eventual judgment, because it would benefit all the possible recipients of the rule, present and future, would end up having the same subjective and objective effectiveness as a judgment in a concentrated control action. In this example, the measure contained in the request formulated in the lawsuit - for the Union to refrain from charging a tax - is nothing more than a natural effect (which does not even imply an express request), which would result from the granting of the direct action of unconstitutionality. The normative precept in question, which created the tax, would end up deprived of any ability to apply both in the specific case and in future cases, in other words, it would be excluded from the legal system, as if it had been declared illegitimate in abstract control.

In view of these considerations, the legislator himself seems to have wanted to avoid them when he added a single paragraph to Article 1 of Law No. 7.347/85, declaring that a public civil action cannot be brought for claims involving taxes, social security contributions, the Severance Indemnity Fund (FGTS) or other funds of an institutional nature whose beneficiaries can be individually determined. Furthermore, by setting territorial limits on the effectiveness of the judgment (which will only cover the defendants who, on the date the action is filed, are domiciled within the territorial jurisdiction of the issuing body), art. 2-A of Law No. 9.494/97[73] (amending the LACP) has made it remote that such effectiveness will have a scope similar to that of a judgment in abstract control. However, the possible occurrence of the hypothesis mentioned above would mean an inadmissible deformation of the system of concentrated control of

---

Coletiva de Direito. 5ª Ed. Sao Paulo: Editora Revista dos Tribunais, 2011. p. 230 to 231.

[73] Art. 2º-A of Law 9.494/97: "A civil judgment handed down in a collective action brought by an association, in defense of the interests and rights of its members, shall only cover the defendants who, on the date the action was brought, were domiciled within the territorial jurisdiction of the issuing body."

constitutionality, which should be repelled .[74]

5.2 - UNCONSTITUTIONALITY AS AN INCIDENTAL ISSUE

The mixed system of constitutionality control adopted in Brazil allows the legitimacy of normative precepts to be controlled simultaneously by incidental means (concrete and diffuse control) and by direct action, the jurisdiction for which is concentrated in the Federal Supreme Court or, as the case may be, in the Courts of Justice of the States and the Federal District, and the initiative of which is restricted to the legitimates described in Article 103 of the Federal Constitution. In the first case, the examination of constitutionality is carried out as a basis for making a judgment on the certainty of the legal relationship and, as such, its binding force is limited to the scope of the specific case itself. In the second case, the declaration of unconstitutionality of the rule represents the very object of the claim, which means that the judgment on the merits implies the recognition of its validity or invalidity with universal subjective efficacy *(erga omnes)* and also universal binding effect .[75]

Also in public civil actions, popular actions and collective actions, the legal rule is not the object but the basis of the decision. There is no obstacle to its constitutionality or unconstitutionality being investigated incidentally within these limits, assessing whether or not the rule is capable of affecting the facts and producing the corresponding legal effects[76] . Such an investigation is typical of diffuse control of constitutionality, which can and should be carried out by any judge, in any case, even ex officio.

[74] Ibid., p. 232.

[75] Ibid., p. 230 to 231.

[76] Jurisprudence of the STF formed from the judgment, on 03.09.1997, of Reclamapoes 600-0/SP, Pleno, rel. Min. Neri da Silveira, DJ 05.12.2003, and 602-6m rel. Min. Ilmar Galvao, Pleno, DJ 14.02.2003. In both cases, it was considered that the incidental control in the public civil action does not imply usurpation of the STF's jurisdiction, since (a) the object of the protection in the public civil action is not the same as that of the direct action, in which it could never be achieved; and (b) the decisions are, in any case, subject to final control by the STF.

5.3 - PUBLIC CIVIL ACTION AND DIRECT ACTION FOR UNCONSTITUTIONALITY

The public civil action and the direct action for unconstitutionality are two different constitutional actions with different objectives. The first acts at the level of constitutional jurisdiction aimed at protecting diffuse and collective rights, and the second at the level of constitutional jurisdiction with the aim of declaring a rule unconstitutional or constitutional in order to guarantee the positive legal order.

In the PCA, unconstitutionality can only be argued as an incidental issue, prejudicial to the judgment on the merits. This is because the public civil action presupposes a collective dispute to be resolved by the judiciary. On the other hand, unconstitutionality as the main issue must be the subject of an ADI, to be brought before the STF by those entitled under Article 103 of the CRFB/88. The object of the public civil action is the protection of the good of life protected by the legal order, and may be based on the unconstitutionality of a law or normative act, posed as a preliminary question, a necessary premise for the judgment of the merits. The object of the declaration of unconstitutionality is the abstract declaration of the unconstitutionality of a law or normative act, with its removal from the system .[77]

As a question prejudicial to the merits, the incidental declaration of unconstitutionality of a rule in a PCA does not become res judicata, in accordance with art. 469, III of the CPC, unlike what happens in a direct action, in which only the declaration of unconstitutionality of the rule becomes res judicata, because this is the very object of the action.

It should be noted that the *erga omnes* effect, when dealing with diffuse rights and individual rights, is proper to both supports, and it is true that in collective action the effect can be national, regional or local, depending on the extent and indivisibility of the damage, not reaching the prejudicial question of

---

[77] SA, Jose Adonis Callou de Araujo. **Public Civil Action and Control of Constitutionality**. p. 144.

unconstitutionality. In turn, a declaration of unconstitutionality in a direct action is res judicata *erga omnes* within the special scope of validity of the impugned law or normative act (national or state) .[78]

In abstract control through direct action, the decision declaring a rule unconstitutional has the effect of removing it from the legal system. However, it does not affect the good of life claimed by the parties .[79]

In view of these considerations, it should be emphasized that the public civil action acts at the level of facts, notably through condemnatory, executive and mandamus injunctions, which ensure its material effectiveness. The direct action for unconstitutionality, on the other hand, is merely declaratory in nature and is limited to suspending the effectiveness of the law or normative act in question .[80]

5.4 - ANALYZING THE CASE IN COURT

It is important to emphasize that the public civil action should not be aimed at declaring unconstitutionality per se. What has not been accepted, however, is the use of public or collective civil action to attack, in the abstract, the *erga omnes* effects, current and future, of a supposedly unconstitutional rule, because in doing so, in the final analysis, the judge of the public or collective civil action would be invading the constitutional attribution of the Courts to which it is exclusively incumbent to declare the unconstitutionality in theory of a law or normative act, to then be provoked, the suspension of its effectiveness, with *erga omnes* immutability .[81]

What is certain is that the specific case will determine the series of situations in which the control of constitutionality in the public civil action should

---

78 QUINTO, Joseane Ribeiro Viana. **The incidental declaration of constitutionality control in public civil action**.
79 SCHAFER, Gilberto. **Public Civil Action and Control of Constitutionality.** p. 126 and 127.
80 QUINTO, Joseane Ribeiro Viana. **The incidental declaration of constitutionality control in public civil action**.
81 MAZZILLE, Hugu Nigro. **The defense of diffuse interests in court: environment, consumer, cultural heritage, public heritage and other interests.** p. 117.

be admitted[82] . The issue began to be discussed after a lawsuit was filed jointly by film companies against the São Paulo State Treasury, with a request for an injunction based on the unconstitutionality of a state law that required students to sell tickets at half price. The plaintiffs wanted to be released from the obligation to sell tickets designated as half-price, on the grounds that the law was unconstitutional, as it violated articles 5, I and IV and 170 of the Federal Constitution .[83]

Analyzing the case above, it can be seen that there was hardly any real conflict of interest to be resolved by the judiciary, since there was no subjective conflict, no duty on the part of the Treasury to inspect and, finally, there was a request for the law to be declared unconstitutional[84] . In fact, only when the law produces concrete effects can its constitutionality be questioned *incidenter tantum*, otherwise it would be a question of challenging a law in theory, which seems to be the case here, where the defendant has not carried out any act based on the law[85] . Thus, in the case in question, the usurpation of the STF's competence for the abstract control of constitutionality appears to have been characterized .[86]

It is worth mentioning an example in which it would be imperative to admit a constitutionality control in ordinary actions such as the public civil action. If the public administration monitored the application of the law and, as a result, came to fine companies that were not charging students only half-price admission, the film companies could go to court and ask for the fine imposed on the basis of the unconstitutional law to be annulled. In this case, it would be clear that the unconstitutionality of the state law had been claimed *incidenter tantum* as a

---

[82] SCHAFER, Gilberto. **Public Civil Action and Control of Constitutionality.** p. 126 and 127,

[83] BRAZIL, SUPREME FEDERAL COURT (Full Court). Rcl. No. 434/SP, Min. Attorney General of the Republic and Judges of Law of the 2ª and 3ª courts of the Public Treasury in the district of Sao Paulo. Rapporteur Minister Francisco Resek J. 10 dec. 1993 **Revista Trimestral de Jurisprudencia** , Brasilia , v. 154, n. 1, p. 13-21.

[84] SCHAFER, Gilberto. **Public Civil Action and Control of Constitutionality.** p. 121.

[85] BRAZIL, SUPREME FEDERAL COURT (Full Court). Rcl. No. 434/SP. . Rapporteur Minister Francisco Resek J. 10 dec. 1993 **Revista Trimestral de Jurisprudencia** , Brasilia , v. 154, n. 1, p. 13-21.

[86] SCHAFER, Gilberto. **Public Civil Action and Control of Constitutionality.** p. 121.

preliminary issue to the merits of the case. If the students, through their representative bodies, also filed a public civil action to force cinema companies to charge half-price tickets, with an injunction, the companies could claim, in their defense, that the state law that established it was unconstitutional. In these two situations, there could be no usurpation of the Supreme Court's competence for the abstract control of constitutionality, since there would be a dispute to be resolved by the removal or application of the unconstitutional law .[87]

5.5 - THE UNDERSTANDING OF THE SUPREME FEDERAL COURT

This is to say that there are certain normative precepts that cannot be subject to abstract control of constitutionality, which is why a judgment in a public civil action, even if it were to have universal subjective effect, could not be considered to be usurping the jurisdiction of the Supreme Court or the Courts of Justice. This is the case when the alleged unconstitutionality, invoked as the basis of the claim, is a municipal law in breach of the Federal Constitution. A direct action for the unconstitutionality of a municipal law does not lie before the STF (art. 102, I, a, CRFB/88). As for the Court of Justice, what is admissible before it is a direct action for the unconstitutionality of a municipal or state law in the face of the State Constitution (art. 125, p. 2 of the CRFB/88), but not when an offense against the Federal Constitution is alleged.

It may happen that the alleged unconstitutionality of the municipal provision is due to an offense against a provision of the state constitution that reproduces a provision of the Federal Charter. In this case too, the offense, if present, is first and foremost the latter, and not the state constitution itself. In such cases, the STF's case law admits the filing of a direct action for unconstitutionality before the local Court of Justice, with the possibility of an extraordinary appeal if the interpretation of the state constitutional rule, which reproduces the federal rule that must be observed by the states, contradicts the

[87] Ibid., p. 121.

meaning and scope of this .[88]

As you can see, for the same reasons that the STF considers that there is no usurpation of its jurisdiction in this direct action by the State Court, it can be said that there is no usurpation of the jurisdiction of the Court of Justice by the first degree judge who tries a public civil action or collective action, even if it has *erga omnes* effect. On the other hand, in the case of a dismissal (such as recognition of the constitutionality of the normative provision by the first degree judge), even if the loser does not challenge the judgment by voluntary appeal, it will still not constitute an obstacle to any direct action for unconstitutionality of the law before the Court of Justice. In this case too, there is no question of invading the domain of concentrated control or of usurping the jurisdiction of the Court of Justice .[89]

The Federal Supreme Court has recognized the legitimacy of using the public civil action as a suitable instrument for the incidental review of the constitutionality, by the diffuse route, of any laws or acts of the Public Power, even when challenged in the face of the Constitution of the Republic, provided that, in this collective process, the constitutional controversy, far from being identified as the sole object of the demand, qualifies as a simple prejudicial question, indispensable to the resolution of the main litigation .[90]

Corroborating the above, the STF's understanding is that the control of constitutionality can be admitted in public civil actions, provided that the questioned rule is in the cause of action and not in the petition. Thus, it is understood that when the STF makes its decision, the declaration will be made in the grounds of the decision, and not in the operative part. Therefore, as only the operative part is res judicata, only this part of the judgment (which does not

---

[88] STF, Full Bench (majority), Rcl. 383-3, rel. Min. Moreira Alves, DJ 21.05.1993.
[89] ZAVASCKI, Teori Albino. **Processo Coletivo - Tutela de Direitos Coletivos e Tutela Coletiva de Direito.** 5ª Ed. Sao Paulo: Editora Revista dos Tribunals, 2011. p. 231 to 233.
[90] RE No. 424993 / DF Full Court Reporting Justice Joaquim Barbosa. Judgment on 12-09-2007. Public civil action and diffuse control (transcripts) Rcl n° 1.733-sp (preliminary injunction)* Rapporteur: Minister Celso de Mello Ementa: Public civil action. Incidental control of constitutionality. Question referred for a preliminary ruling. Possibility. No usurpation of the federal supreme court's jurisdiction.

contain the declaration of unconstitutionality) will have *erga omnes* effect, since the aforementioned Article 16 of Law 7.347/85 states that the civil judgment will be res judicata *erga omnes* .[91]

5.6 - PUBLIC CIVIL ACTION AS AN INSTRUMENT OF DIFFUSE CONTROL OF CONSTITUTIONALITY

As you can see, the public civil action is a typical constitutional action aimed at protecting fundamental rights provided for in the Constitution of the Federative Republic of Brazil. As such, its interpretation must always seek the effectiveness of constitutional norms .[92]

In the same vein, based on Canotilho's doctrine, he points out that public civil action is a constitutional *writ* for the enforcement of fundamental rights, and in this sense the principle of maximum effectiveness should be extended in its interpretation .[93]

We must therefore seek a constitutional interpretation that recognizes public civil action's important constitutional role as a right - a guarantee, the one that instrumentalizes the protection of fundamental rights. To consider that the issue of constitutionality control cannot be dealt with in public civil action, as a preliminary issue, is tantamount to minimizing or even destroying the

---

[91] Public civil action filed by the Public Ministry of the Federal District with multiple requests, including a request for a declaration of unconstitutionality incidenter tantum of District Law 754/1994, which regulates the occupation of public places in the Federal District. The question of order raised by the rapporteur was resolved in the sense that the declaration of unconstitutionality of Law 754/1994 by the Court of Justice of the Federal District does not render the extraordinary appeal null and void due to loss of purpose. The case law of the Federal Supreme Court has recognized that it is possible to claim the unconstitutionality of a given normative act in a public civil action, as long as it is incidenter tantum. However, the use of public civil action to achieve a declaration of unconstitutionality with erga omnes effects is prohibited. In this case, the request for a declaration of unconstitutionality of Law 754/1994 is merely incidental, constituting a real cause of action. The Federal District's extraordinary appeal was dismissed and the extraordinary appeal filed by the Public Ministry of the Federal District was dismissed.

[92] BARROSO, Luis Roberto. **Interpretation and application of the constitution.** Sao Paulo: Saraiva, 1996. p. 218.

[93] CANOTILHO, J J Gomes. **Constitutional Law**, Coimbra: Almedina, 1993, p. 227

effectiveness of this mechanism for protecting fundamental rights. .[94]

In view of the above, we must emphasize the search for an interpretation that does not prejudice the use of public civil action in the sphere of collective and diffuse rights, under the terms of the Federal Constitution, which is why public civil action, like any ordinary action, must be able to deal with diffuse constitutionality control, without the decision handed down in this preliminary question having *erga omnes* effectiveness .[95]

Finally, it should be emphasized that the control of constitutionality exercised in the public civil action is diffuse control that can be exercised through any action brought before the judiciary.

---

[94] FARIAS, Paulo Jose Leite. **Public civil action and constitutionality control**. p.
[95] FARIAS, Paulo Jose Leite. **Public civil action and constitutionality control**. p. 3

6. CONCLUSION

Public civil action is a constitutional action aimed at protecting fundamental *latu senso* or transindividual collective rights, defined in infra-constitutional legislation as *strictu senso* collective rights, diffuse rights and homogeneous individual rights.

At the same time as it provides, among other things, for public civil action as an instrument of collective protection, the Constitution of the Federative Republic of Brazil follows a very peculiar model with regard to the control of constitutionality exercised in the country, given the coexistence of incidental diffuse control and principal control.

The control of constitutionality is proper to judicial activity, since it can be carried out by any judge or court in order to resolve a conflict of interests brought before it. The constitutional issue in this case is indispensable to the judgment of the case and must be decided as a preliminary issue on the merits. Once the unconstitutionality of the rule has been recognized, this decision will only affect the parties to the case and will have *ex tunc* (retroactive) effect, rendering null and void any legal relationship based on the unconstitutional rule from the outset.

Respecting the differences between the two institutes, including the purpose of each action, there is no need to speak of usurping the competence of the STF for the abstract control of constitutionality when in the collective action the unconstitutionality of a normative text is argued.

At the end of the day, it is hoped that this work has served to clarify the issue and encourage further research, since it was not intended to exhaust the study, nor even to put an end to the controversy surrounding the viability of constitutionality control in public civil action.

7. BIBLIOGRAPHICAL REFERENCES

. **Public civil action: reminiscences and reflections after 10 years of application.** 1ª Ed. Sao Paulo: Revista dos Tribunals, 1995. AGRA, Walber de Moura. **Manual of Constitutional Law**. Sao Paulo: Revista dos Tribunals, 2002.

BARROSO, Luis Roberto. **Curso de Direito Constitucional Contemporaneo: Os conceitos Fundamentais e a constituigao do novo modelo.** 2nd Ed. Sao Paulo: Saraiva, 2010.

BARROSO, Luis Roberto. **The Control of Constitutionality in Brazilian Law.** 6th Ed. Sao Paulo: Saraiva, 2012.

BONAVIDES, Paulo. **Constitutional Law Course.** 11th Ed. Sao Paulo: Malheiros, 2001.

BRAZIL, **Constitution of the Federative Republic of Brazil**, of October 5, 1988. 47th Ed. Sao Paulo: Saraiva, 2012.

BRASILIA, Supreme Court. STF News. In: Hybrid model of constitutional control guarantees more speed for Brazilian justice. Available at: **<http://www.stf.ius.br/portal/cms/verNoticiaDetalhe.asp7id Conteudo=115824>** Accessed on: 10 jun. 2012.

BRAZIL, Law No. 6.938, of August 31, 1981. Provides for the National Environmental Policy, its purposes and formulation and application mechanisms, and other measures. Available at: http://www.planalto.gov.br/ccivil_03/leis/l6938.htm. Accessed on March 27, 2013.

BRAZIL, Law No. 8.078, of September 11, 1990. Provides for consumer protection and other measures. **Consumer protection and defense code.** Brasilia Ministry of Justice, 2001. Available at: http://www.planalto.gov.br/ccivil_03/leis/l8078.htm. Accessed on March 27, 2013.

BRAZIL, Law No. 9.868, of November 10, 1999. Provisions on the process and judgment of direct actions of unconstitutionality and declaratory actions of constitutionality before the Federal Supreme Court. Available at:

http://www.planalto.gov.br/ccivil_03/leis/l9868.htm. Accessed on March 27, 2013.

CLEVE, Clemerson Merlin. **A fiscalizapao abstrata da constitucionalidade do direito brasileiro**. 2ªed. Sao Paulo: Revista dos Tribunais, 2000.

FARIAS, Paulo Jose Leite. Public civil action and constitutionality control. **Jornal da Associapao do Ministerio Publico do Distrito Federal e Territorios.** Brasilia, n° 16 jan./feb./mar. 2001.

GRINOVER, Ada Pellegrini *et al.* **Codigo brasileiro de defesa do consumidor.** 7th Ed. Rio de Janeiro: Forense Universitaria, 2001.

MAZZILLE, Hugu Nigro. **The defense of diffuse interests in court: environment, consumer, cultural heritage, public heritage and other interests.** 15 Ed. Sao Paulo: Saraiva, 2002.

MENDES, Gilmar Ferreira. **Jurisdipao Constitucional:** o controle abstrato de normas no Brasil e na Alemanha. 3rd Ed. Sao Paulo: Saraiva, 1999.

MENDES, Aluisio Gonpalves de Castro. **Collective Support in Comparative and National Law.** 2nd Ed. Sao Paulo: Revista dos Tribunais, 2010.

MILARE, Edis. **The Public Civil Action after 20 years: effectiveness and challenges.** 1st Ed. Sao Paulo: Revista dos Tribunais, 2005.

MORAES, Alexandre de. **Constitutional Law.** 21st Ed. Sao Paulo: Atlas, 2007.

MOREIRA, Barbosa. **Themes of Brazilian procedural law.** 1ª Ed. Sao Paulo: Saraiva, 1977.

. **The control of constitutionality in law**

Brasileiro. 6th Ed. Sao Paulo: Saraiva, 2012.

PADILHA, Rodrigo. **Systematized Constitutional Law.** 2aed. Rio de Janeiro: Forense, 2012.

QUINTO, Joseane Ribeiro Viana. **The incidental declaration of constitutionality control in a public civil action**. Belo Horizonte: Del Rey, 2002.

REALE, Miguel. **LiQdes preliminares de direito.** 27th Ed. Sao Paulo: Saraiva, 2002.

RUSSO, Luciana. **Direito de Constitucionalidade,** 5th Ed. Sao Paulo: Saraiva,

2012.

SA, Jose Adonis Callou de Araujo. **A$ao Civil Publica e Controle de Constitucionalidade**. Belo Horizonte: Del Rey, 2002.

SILVA, Jose Afonso da. **Course in positive constitutional law**. 18 Ed. Sao Paulo: Malheiros, 2000.

ZAVASCKI, Teori Albino. **Processo Coletivo - Tutela de Direitos Coletivos e Tutela Coletiva de Direitos.** Sao Paulo: Revista dos Tribunais, 2011.

MIX
Papier aus verantwortungsvollen Quellen
Paper from responsible sources
FSC® C105338

Printed by Books on Demand GmbH, Norderstedt / Germany